LIMITS AND TRIALS

Contemporaries
Robert Hazel, Editor

LIMITS AND TRIALS

by

Henry Birnbaum

New York University Press
New York   1970

Library of Congress Catalogue Card Number: 77-133023

ISBN: 0-8147-0962-1

Manufactured in the United States of America

One or more of these poems appeared previously in the following
publications: *Arts and Sciences; Beloit Poetry Journal; Carolina
Quarterly; Carleton Miscellany; Chicago Review; Chrysalis;
Coastlines; Compass Review; Fiddlehead; Golden Year; Human-
ist; Inland; Literary Review; Morning Star; New Poetry Pamphlets;
Olivant; Poems and Pictures; The Poet; Poetry; San Francisco Ae-
view; Sewanee Review; Sparrow Magazine; Talisman; Whetstone;
Western Humanities Review; Wormwood Review.*

CONTENTS

FROM THE GARDEN

On a certain morning, the woman
bends to throw some Rinso in her cart.
A spot is on her breast. It will not
wash but grows insane. She listens
as she counts her change. The man who
owns the next counter is louder
than the colored shirt he wears.
He sounds like bread and herring.
The shelves are full of suds and names.
The woman pauses, fits her gloves
and walks through the swinging door.

The road is wet and whispers under.
The man rides a white line narrowing
his eyes. He is nearsighted. Cars
and trees row past his mind. He listens
with his foot on the treadle. The voice
comes honeyed and hoarse. It strings
across space and is carefully entertaining.
The sound is made of skin and teeth.
A billboard crashes into the eye. He leans
forward, fingers the wheel lightly
and looks to the palm in the distance.

The window makes a pattern on chenille.
She lingers on her nails wondering how
the hand foretells. Her thoughts erupt
in blemishes. Beside the bed, the stand
invents a world of lovers. The afternoon
beckons to the bride. She makes herself
a month of pages. Between the words, she
makes his voice in leather. He could be
rich and promising. And now the picture
of the summer house, and her finger
held out shining for the ring.

Two simple chairs approach a Braque.
The man holds a chin on an arm. He
has a tie that makes a part of the room.
There in that cubic blend of motionless
color he listens to the absence of sound.
The silence has the thickness of walls.
Whose mind hangs seeking a balance
of line and love. The forms require
penitence. He approaches a moment of brown,
examines its texture, and turns his head
towards the tinkle of glasses.

Mosaic tiles sit together under the moon.
They hold a memory not of their design. She
comes through the curtains with a cough. Her
hand is white. Inside the voice winds round
its wax home. It has the sound of wire
and paper leaves. A man must be explicit.
What he says is almost what he means. Even
a recording can avoid itself. She listens
against a brace of stone. Footsteps turn
the corner. She looks up, smiles whitely
and prepares herself for talk.

On a certain evening, the man
brushes the lint from his serge. It is
a nervous gesture. He carries it inside.
He listens to the water in the kitchen.
Glasses must have the transparency of sin.
The room has been arranged. A voice enters
like some imitation of silk. He listens
bending over the tray. She has the sound
of creams and canapes. The beads
set off the breast. He thinks it time
to laugh and make himself appropriate.

LIVING

Known streets become
time become words
and are called
environment

but the lie of that
becomes psychology
and truth turns
the corner

thus friendship
is that good turn
out of time
where

I look up
from my accounts
becoming wisdom
and say

what if he dies
then how shall I
proceed with
living.

TOUCHING

Related
to objects like red
vases on tables,
like trees in dark
luxuries of night,

that strung energy
whispered in space,
wished on time
kissed
by hands.

She
swings around
the swing of the door
in silk
to my sight.

She is
she before closets,
and I am nervously
touching air
about her.

ESPECIALLY
Simply defined
it is the tinkling bell
that opened
the candy store

after
going past
the steam jet out
from the tailor's

and stopping
to look down the grill
where wrappers had
collected.

The bell
comes
with
Mr. Forman
again.

THE FALL OF THE SECOND NATIONAL TRUST

1.

We played chinese handball beneath the gilded heals,
five or six of us, bent and agile, meeting ourselves
in the washed speckled marble, nimbly reflected
on the thick torso of stone like a child's drawings,
guarding our cement squares against a bouncing ball.
The eagle, gazing from its golden frieze, assigned
a blank resentment to our elastic ease
as if our thin knees were deftly disrespectful
of a sturdy dignity, like an organ grinder
winding his pleasantries in a hospital zone.
The game was slight and in its slightness heresy,
our scores chalked on the walls, irreverent
as scratched whims upon palace decorations.
The windows, long and properly recessed, overlooked
vulgarity like sentinels about a sacred place.

2.

Inside there was a sense of iron and glass
entered through a hush of revolving doors
then enclosed as if our thoughts were known
and all our movements adequately assessed.
We were uniformed in a shyness rejected
by polished brass, a break in conversations
spilled upon the settled state, a charity
given by calculated consent, an ungifted coin
on the floor of cubicles, a whisper commerced
like untruths sanctioned by the temple.
We were those nameless necessary evils
that turn about the pestilence of precision
like so many cubits applied to the wavering
balance of the last light bill.

3.

We were a fiction, a toss up of urchins
scattered about those formal transactions,
a wander of myths unconsciously staged
like a neighborhood drama against stone
and document, that nameless unreason
that swarms about civilizations
and become the children of ballads.
We were an awkward chorus of change,
a roaming maypole spending banners,
frivolous and unrecorded, like summer birds
nesting among the statues in city parks,
a generation of defeat and return,
chased and growing and seemingly aimless
within that disbursed array of busyness.

4.

Yet the theme should have been familiar,
a repeated arrangement of sand tunneled
by significance and kicked by the seasons.
We were allied in weakness and change,
webbed in revolt against all structures,
the stone haunched and towering prides
labelled like ministers who display duty
or like efficient botanical gardens
where visitors press hands to their sides
and admire the thorough abundance of orchids.
We owned our shares of honor, dividends
of unborrowed birth, the passion of growth
pushing over the mass of columned marble
in a challenge of youngness with arrogance
and all the tenderness of a first crime.

5.

The victory came last, clank rolling
down the street in a wonder of destruction,
a swinging giant shattering tenements
with holes in the skeletons of emptiness,
destroying an unwhimpering slum heart.
We watched bleacher-eyed the scarred
effigies of buildings, a brittle borough
shedding its landscape, rumble of bricks
falling clattering on a no man's field.
There remained only the marbled memory
in the rubble of emptied shells,
a chalked headstone rendering a city
like the remains of an unused monastery,
an atrophy of consecrated gestures.

6.

We moved away from its standing loneliness
and played at growth in another part of town.

ROUSSEAU'S LION

My doorstep makes the sun civil,
lying there like odalisque in ready
reality, this polite and coughing Sunday
when all the pallid pavement weeps
for morning bells and forgotten mailmen.

And the polished children characterize
this venice of artificiality with whiteness.
See how their ankles are covered with white
and careful socks, how the sun reflects
from their patent leather walk.

I think to pluck an orange flower
and petal it in the shade.

Rousseau's lion comes kittening through
a vase of thick tropical underbrush
with large and primitive paws hidden
in an overgrowth of cynical green spears
looking much like Bert Lahr at his best.

A PART OF IT

The darkness lies in pools
in the corner of
the room
there
where
in darkness crawls
an insect.

The curtain
having been hung grey
and yellow
on the side of
the sun
remains occasionally
lifted by air.

Outside somewhere
to the right of the eye
red climbers
make neighbors of
the house
across green lawns
and traffic.

But there I
am making sight
the invasion of
streets and
growth
knowing well that seeing
is a part of it.

AMIELY

Face down in her black sea,
she lost our mind, loving her—
self in a float of history.

Morning rose on her mind.
It was in light of her,
the spray of sun defined

the moment of her hair.
She came awake among brown
manufactories and care—

less restaurants where
windows give local reason.
Between elevator and stair

she fell a quarter century
to obstruct city traffic
with today's anonymity.

LOCAL TO CATHEDRAL

1. Morning at the Mirror

Behind the mirror, the bottles like Cezanne's peaches
await the light. The sun invades the air. The eyes
are large, and the skin touches where the hand
reaches for the chin. The bottles remain cool.

More a park than a single tree, the sun caresses
a blouse of green, like a stagelight follows thoughts.
O curious vaudeville that makes growing the focus
of standing at the ledge. Here is a tomboy tree
wearing an iron frame. One must not call this wisdom.

In this corner is the mirror image rolling the eyes
to loosen the daylight. Now we can appreciate the voice
of water from the tap. It has a true wet way
of measuring reality. The referee leans towards soap.
We hear the morning frying and hang towels on the news.
We feel the scrape of chairs, the double knot on our shoes.

2. The Headlines

Pity the poor city planner who drops a stitch of iron
and spreads his blueprints on the floor trying to find
his name in time for the next board meeting while
a hundred thousand tokens march through turnstiles
and a union spokesman says he's tired of promises
and the mayor hasn't taken a position yet.

What makes them want to tame a circus with words
prancing down the feature page in between lions
and the lady with thongs wound round her calves: the idea
of a carload of sawdust coming on barges and keepers
and roustabouts making elephants feel at home.

Daddies ought to have a way of knowing when
their daughters are getting cosmetic and sort of
ripe legged. Why is it always a surprise with eyes
bulging out of their foreheads and sweat coming down
when a cop calls to ask do you have a big girl.

3.   In Communal Transit

The principal jest of Peter is discovery. We rush
through mortuarial caverns seeking light.

Thoreau was claustrophobic and quietly desperate
seeking to move out of his neighborhood, never
divining motion as progress.

Huzzah, the city shifts its weight.

The shuttle lights its wobbling pain through
faces like echoes in chewing gum mirrors
thrust rushing into desire with its long car
stretching to the ends of reality. The stab of light
reaches out and cuts a crumble of bodies.

What statistical invention made this metropolis?
How with numbers commuting across electric impulses
we make regular measurements of time.

What daring Americus standing on the deck said here?
What pinchpennyed churchgoing trader and general store
keeper knew he'd found a gold mine?

4.   The Carpenter Finds a Place

Comes now the artisan with mystery packed in his
black lunchbox with fig newtons for his friends when
he sits down with his square on the ground self
effacing and wholly reluctant to say he knows the
weariness of daylight and the crush of nails.

He's eyeless and nevertheless. The people own him
and send him through boroughs to surface on the wish
and joist of regeneration. He sits upon the average
between the dull and dying and says what am I but
a carpenter who makes his hands stigmata.

5.   The Student Plans His Honor

Whereas having satisfactorily completed the requirements
and in recognition of the competitive adornment of our
time, we do hereby ascend to the uppermost level where
we shall accept leadership and with due regard for
what has gone before begin to articulate.

6.   Sermon

We are in perpetual transit in the service
of our deeds, the lights changing tell us where.
And when He sits beside you, brethren,
do not stop to ask His Destination.

7.   Sermon

You will note that our agreement is precise.
I was to deliver in exchange. There is no room
for hesitation. The ethics are clear. Decisions
must travel in one direction. Please be so good
as to review the invoice and forward your check.

8.   Sermon

We have come to understand the ascent of the species
more precisely. Dominated by forces beyond even
animal will, spurred on by centuries of survival and
sport, spared by the way the earth tilts and the planets
move, we have invaded space with an astounding skill
and shaped clay and learned to communicate across time.

9. From Within

Timeclock and memory where tweed and cotton explorers
look up at street numbers and wonder what primordial
event disgorged me here.

Eventful is this overflow: staccato of continental
divides: deliberate subterranean cauldron and melting
pot bubbling over with jingles and trademarks.

What hour of parkbenches and sunlight paraded before
and sold me a revolution to own? What statue
rising out of the soil invented me?

Suddenly windows are hurt by pushing reflections.

EIGHT SKETCHES FROM A CROWDED POOLROOM

1. Aaron, The Encyclopaedia

Effigy of thought:
his bald head strung across the line of sight,
mockery of arrested time, cue for laughter
which is the pride of resentment
> *C'mere you psycho bastard* (no sympathy for
> the sad clown) *the world is full of balls,*
> *balls.*

He refuses to be clinical. They lean across
their shots, marking the ricochets of sly
togetherness (the sad clown among his friends),
a falling together and yet torn apart
by that one terrible opening thrust. Failing
failing file of lost intelligence. How cruel.
To find the rules of the game
> arranged in the house.

2. Chick-Eagle-Eye

Do not lay odds on his docility. He knows.
He lives with mirrors in his mind, reflections
of the slightest innuendo, angles of judgment
banked against a wall of experience.
> *Hey, call your shots* (never trust the
> prestidigitator) *give me the number and*
> *name the pocket.*

He keeps truth to masse friendship. Love
and truth roll out of a dark bottle. They watch
the finesse of his movement (legerdemain open
for admiration), the magician performs
in isolation. The prodigy poises his baton,
adjusts himself to display, and spills contempt
upon the situation.

3. Kismet, The Miser

Tall and alone, his sunken cheeks prove
the economy of his features, never risking
courage but that careful estimate of what remains,
treasurer of deception
>Nobody gets conned (the thin man is on
>the inside) like the guy who's scared to lose
>>his money.

He never laughs unless it counts. They bring him
to the rack with cunning, turning his body
under the sadistic heat (the thin freak in a fat
and sloppy world) of smiles. And reviewing
his claim for reconsideration, they agree
that he is the victim of chance. What luck.
That he must submit his caution
>>to trick exhibitions.

4. Lennie, The Doc

Sickness personified:
he sniffs at his addiction before he speaks,
drugged argument of a jaded world, pipe dream
disarrayed about his weakness
>You got holes in your arm (see the man with
>the artificial heart) like the holes in your
>>head.

That index to hypochondria, losing his senses
to the hypnotic play, the twitching body bends
across the table (his mind a cynical operation).
Somewhere in the stimulated clarity of the game,
he steps up for his turn, looks nobly about
at the amateurs and bends his perfect control
to the sure amazement of the shot.

5. Loverboy Tony

His cuff links shine like kings. Harmony
of sensual motion portrayed like a hero
masculine before the eyes of men, smooth
ardor of the lewd ambition
     When he calls 'em (meet the only siamese
      attached to his sister) *they come sucking*
                       and crawling.
The lurid adventure is part of the game, between
turns, when they stand honing their cues
like men in the back alley (his pants are tight
against his things) waiting to engage desire.
Enter the trapeze artist whose body is his soul,
with muscle somersaulting across the bars
of vicarious destiny.

6. Dark Sam

His eyes are dark with laconic anger. Doom
sheathed like the dagger but ready for devotion
he makes his profit from terror: danger
provides for its keeper
     Give back six for five (don't you wish you
      could be a fire eater) or *hide behind your*
                       old lady.
He may be affected by the movies, that swagger
of pent-up action, still he is essentially pure,
a threat (fire eaters never speak to strangers)
which has its proper place. Fear stands
in the corner and marks their flaws in his book,
a diary of fools who spend their energy
over the clicking
               break of the rack.

7.   Tommy, The Count

This one is a special sort, a royal remnant
thriving on exile. He is partly a lie,
an exaggeration returned from enforced reform,
training achieves its polish
      He come back from up there (let's go to
        the center ring) *and up there they learned him*
                          how.
No one cheats him, but it is a victory to win
his confidence, a satellite of convicted glory
beaming (some are born to leaders and others
spend their lives as followers). Inversion
of romance. The villain takes his bows and smiles,
proud to be the main event, the disappearing act
reappears to share their cheers.

8.   Buggsy

What is his name, those eyes which have lost
their sanity, that voice which seeks its own
coherence. Sometimes the game is play,
and often a deadly challenge
      Here we go round and round (everybody
      laughs at monkeys) *and back we come*
                        as fairies.
He thinks he knows. They stand around
and whisper while he shoots, the schemers
acting like friends (if you're going to laugh,
then stand before the bars) like alliances
which parade their pleasantness about the inner
voice, the sudden sound which reaches
into the peace that comes with the good shot.

ORIZONS

0.1

Sometimes when
        the eye hangs
on a hook in the closet
(figuratively I mean)
and the sun is
a sheet on the wall,
impertinent is
the arrangement of
          yourself
and mawkish is
the handkerchief
in a white breastpocket,
even Icelandic sagas
and reporters poised
on a newsbreak.
                Listen.
They are talking about
a new
        isomorphic
        dedicated
              soap.

0.2

I know
what they want
            words
that squint
making distance
        an abstraction.
Nope.
They want
        words
like confetti (only

real) falling from
your pockets
                    to your shoes,
a number of colored
spots on your shoes,
of words
          an arrangement
          on your shoes
to make a poem.
              They want.

0.3

I ought to thank
          Zukofsky,
a wonderful voice,
          Zukofsky.
That makes me eclectic
wonderfully pejoratively
              eclectic,
but I don't care
and neither should he
should he
          so long as we
walk out on cartels
          and make sounds
that sound uncom
              fort
                    able
in parlor chairs.

0.4

It's contrived.
              Who can
deny that.

27

What would they say
in velvet gowns
would they
            what say
of words
            and the vice
of device.
            It seems to me
that art can love
            its high
seriousness
            too too.

0.5

The effortless
            poses a problem
really.
            Any man becomes
the critic perplexed by
artlessness deceived by
casual assault.
            I think
the brute is genuine
            but should be
chained to view.
            Is this
true
      of the child
at waterfountains?

0.6

I didn't mean
            to mean.
It's nervy you know
to make words
            too wordy.

28

Much better to bounce
                words
up and down
                and count them
and skip round them
                and watch them
come up to the surf
                and wing out
floating higher
                until
they are out of sight
                        pleasantly.

0.7

Should be gestalt
                        breaking
into view like turning
a corner.
You've got to know the price
of words so
                arranged
like matchsticks
                racing down
blood without think-
ing, pamperers of ideas
never coming up
        with overnight operas.
And
        isn't this what they want
to see in anthologies?

0.8

Trees don't say much
                        being
there in the park next to

29

the pipe and chess.
                    Over the
shoulder a bird peoples
                    your move
and spills time.

But
     there on
the watch of your mind
it grows and dies
          and poets know
they're mated.

                    0.9

What is the calling
                    of ponds
suddenly terrifyingly accept-
ingly stilling
                    by the swift
side of the road with its glass
eyes passing by wishing near?
How clean Solomon clean are
its thoughts
               a water and peace
if we
     a great drum of timbre
if we, all of us,
     a great coolness in the
journey, a wetness of whiling
trees and a looking back at us.
It must be an echo.
                    Who calls?

                    0.10

When you consider
                    all those horses

pointed at the sky with their stone
generals,
                you wonder what sentiment
makes the great hero.
A park is a proper thing for words
and checkers: two hands lined move
across muttering squares to make
an audience
                two young heads bring
parks of words.
                And a kid who put
Tom Swift under the bench bends at
the fountain just below the Civil
War
        and drinks it almost cold.

0.11

Something quiet on the wall, a
friend
        had made a friend
                        with
wood and stillness
                with giving
and dexterity. She has carved
eyes and statement out of no-
thingness.
        And she is there
always there
        more than wood
even when I put out the light.

0.12

Libraries
        and their companion
lions loyal through cities
accumulating respect.

                    It is
theirs to arbitrate the traffic
to summer patrol
                    the limber
flow of here and theres.
                                    I
stop at their granite feet,
cats of time.
                    These words
are mine.

                0.13

From whence comes
                    this strength,
my utility in friendship?
My mother made me ever child,
always
            the memory of her hands
at my winter clothes
                clothes the buttons
of my mind.
                And she was warm
in ignorance.
                My father
moved in and out of doorways,
pent upon principle upon
                            a lit
candle and a shadow.
Two boys once
                chased me to a
wall and beat the hell into me.
I forget
            their reason.

0.14

Who can doubt the future,
> boy

with blocks and towers, small
words with large letters, water
> she lost our mind, loving her

for yesterday's him?
> Who can, I can.

Tomorrow is the sun on the roof.
Hooray.
> Tomorrow disagrees.

boards agree.
> Tonight the executive

I don't think I'll ever
> change my mind.

UNSPOKEN

What clarity accompanies the corpse.
The eye in chemical silence
observes the quick.

I fear most the ceremony, the play of public
upon public in behalf of death.

I fear the whispers in their chairs,
the candles.

I fear those few hours of stillness,
the time to be forgotten.

Trees drink water and partake of minerals
without this charge. Friends, believe me,
I leave no soul at large.

NON-EUCLIDEAN

(for William V. Consolazio)

When we lean upon a stool and look,
there is always a kingdom of silence.
I say, it isn't quite.
It seeks defending
hanging there on a broken promise.

Two faces close to color.
The whites should have their right.
They should be pure, cruel and white,
but they are weak and bending.
There is the texture of cream
running through my anger.

The eyes make a path
through a wound in my mind,
and I dislike the illusion of dimension.
The hand shakes us at the ending.
It holds an illness
that breeds a private delight.

Yellow has a courage though.
You would not think it so. It is new
and a challenge to the sight.
The hero captures what is undesigned.
He is a melting of yellow desire,
forever won by attending.

Color is sick with ambition.
It has a way of offending.
I say, the balance gives the cage.
It ways of blue: remain.
What matters in the primaries
when they contain a fear.

A line should be devoted.
It should be allowed to bow in space.
It should move in grace.
Yet a line is like a false word,
never breathing like a bird.
These deficiencies are noted.

BINDING

1. Because the hill is
   some distance
   in my memory,
                how
   does it live to be
   near?

2. Then sun
   of tropic drums and
   laboratory frequencies
   is too brilliant
   to view
             as a point in
   time.

3. Never before were birds
   birds to me,
        and now they are
   thus wing and window
   alive and light.

4. What streets
   will become mine when I
   no longer am:
        those shadows by
   light along the length
   of houses,
            those sounds back

beyond desks of thought
beyond the child who
never saw the wall the
          fence where
I fell and cried
without my
              mother
near.

And she gray
          in the yellow
light when the sun burned
her presence.
          I heard her tell
of once
when she heard soldiers
and ran with her sons
which makes me
want to ask again again
and did you
                    hide
like I did
and cry.

5. This tree now
    green growing in my
    middle years
              and before
    this tree now, host
    to my thoughts and
    gracious
                    with all the
    practice of time.

6. Held by uncertainty
    light and time bending
    become
              the extent and mass
    of mystery.

ON THE DEATH OF MY MOTHER

Who will remember you, rattling your pans
across the rites of eternity. I suppose
your instrument was too immediate, too personal,
to scar the forever mountain. You marched
suitably unknown with the unlimited millions
who appear and disappear over the rolling
cycles of time. And you would have had it so.
Too actual to practice the self-conscious
gestures of heroes, you busied like those
who bleached linens in the sun and counted
daily vegetables for regular tables. Yet
you might have been embarrassed had we forgotten
to gather for some brief display.

Thus, we were seated in a brown room,
thick with the odor of talcum, halting
with candles flickering against our intonations.
You would have had it so,
I resented his gold teeth, the nimble stuttering
of his bought solemnity chasing ministerial
the fading intimations of change. I would have stood,
face to the wall, staining the moment,
like a child separately turning his anger
against love. But we tore our vests
for the occasion and faced one another
to dramatize our courage and rode majestic
the polished limousines to the final melting
into time. You would have had it so.

Yet forgive me that I violate your confidence.
It will not matter in the infinite torque
of heaven that we had meaning for each other.
We were not friends, testing our hopes
against the mythical experience of our days,
but meeting often in misunderstanding,

we were linked by some subterranean flow
of nature. You hoped to guide me to those
common isles where all who live in innocence
accept the simple safeties.
Though I wandered, I reserved your love.

LEAF MOLD

The body
formally arranged with
hands upon its chest
never hears the car
running past
on its way to
Des Moines,

and light comes
surprised
like candles on cake
down cellars
where grey
rats make a perfect circle
round old bread.

Thus
plants so
practice
their asceticism
on the beds
of forest
darkness.

A SENSE OF HUGGING TO ONESELF

1. No one has ever asked the things
   I used to think with my feet dangling
   over the school. I had forgotten
   my thoughts below the kitchen table
   with the sun its distance away. I
   could have been asked how fine
   the future all those avenues and transfers
   away. No one ever asked.

2. Villon, let's polish apples and stack them
   for the marketplace. Our knowledge is
   a cellar weed, something ugly and pure,
   such a cholera of words to infect
   the populace. Let's chalk obscenities
   on city streets, the kind Erasmus knew
   or Baudelaire invented. We'll reproduce
   an epidemic of affection.

3. The corner drugstore pickles its magic.
   Maimonides pinches the cheek, sticks
   his eye into yours, makes a tongue of
   yours, and asks about you and the dark.
   Behind the vials, the mortar and pestle
   revel, and telephone booths are strung
   on pain. The formulae and ciphers
   recommend an opiate for the night's pass.

4. And for you, Miss Boland, whose face
   has disciplined a generation, come
   with me down two flights of orderly stairs
   through a well arranged corridor into
   a dying courtyard. Are you with me, two
   by two with silence that becomes.
   Closer now here the spider's gone and
   the web is dust itself. There: I wrote:
   Fuck you, Miss Boland. And it was good.

5. A chicken plucker ought to have a universe,
   and so he does. The day he sinned, the
   wrinkled skin of heaven was calloused
   and blue and Gold left pinfeathers to scar
   the name. Lady, what have I done to deserve
   an afternoon thick with entrails and tired
   love. What greater gift to receive than
   to place my hand within a silken glove.

6. Next door they sew in undershirts
   and slang. The steam will send a boy
   to Harvard so he can say, look where
   I came. Ten thousand creases to hang
   a shingle on a town green, and he'll say,
   I know what it was to live in greed.
   But it's hot to fit the bust
   and say, my son the doctor.

7. Pigeons must have a union. They feel
   an ownership in the park. O sure
   we clean their coops and wave a wand
   to save ourselves. Imagine how sure
   footed they are, pecking at the Indian
   nuts and leaning over the checker game.
   Suppose they never returned. The quiet.
   The hot roof tar. And the rigid city.

8. Eh, this you'd call a Notre Dame? all
   squeezed and narrowed without the room
   to spread its Christ, with gargoyles
   in rolled up sleeves fanning themselves
   in the windows? Lighting candles is
   no harm, no harm to memorize a thing or two,
   but when the heat rolls down your underarms,
   please God let it be known that I would
   sell my place for a cold pitcher on a roof.

9. The night has only legs, or better the echo
    of steps. You hear them in your bed and
    peek out to see an empty street. You listen
    and they hobble up the hallway stairs. Those
    belong to the fifth floor, all the way up
    to save the rent. A boy and girl and the usual
    shuffle.

    If I could walk along the river
    I would make myself proud and alone for lovers.

FLATLAND

It is the even distance that dulls. Memories remain
in dusty cities and beyond the purple mountains.
Here the land is crossed by tradition. From this house,
decorated with its repair of history, I look out
on fields and fields, afraid of their familiarity
which makes of me another. It is not grimness
which offers up despair, but the reach of yesterdays
in which I am older and less free to change.
Now rocking on the wide landscape, I nod on
yields of time tuned to an endless horizon.
And there in a challenge of sight, the scarecrow,
posed like a drunkard's moonlit laugh,
wishes I had the freedom of birds, if free
they are, bounded by earth and air, by me.
Sun, darkness, and I have become a natural trio
here on this squared off acreage. I see
the furrows move up the afternoon to night
and roll up my thoughts again and again,
remembering where I'd been before these days.

THE GREAT HEART OF LAZAR SHUMSKY

1. A Turn of Mind

The third person is my weakness. And I
but there am faced with more of me.

He is my sleep and fear. He is the lie
and death in the double step of me.

He is my pimpled walk in the metropole
and my sandaled foot in history.

He is my father's eyes and simpled soul
and my other laugh in bartery.

He is perjury and permanence. A gift
of false desire. Exactor of penalty.

He is my mirrored and meaning am. Thrift
of my being and reflex of mystery.

2. To a Mannequin

You, in your waltz of silence, and I,
in my weep of motion, invert the sense,
a soft shoe against the truth, an ache
of movement glazed in advertisement.

Sweet much, want me as you are desired.
Make me humble as the glass beads upon
your beatified breast, and needed as
artificial flowers in a papered world.

Let us, you and I, exchange a wish
across irrevocable distance dedicated
to the premonition and the final
certainty of anonymous leniencies.

3. Synod

In the beginnign was the river, and He
made a wall to keep her in. I remember
the water and the word.

              He has made sun
light become candlelabra. And sound
has He made which is a concert.

There is a day, full of rite, when
we bring us to the waters, and I
come to the wash and turn to the wall
of the city, looking up.

4. Who in a Distant City

Traveler, you who wander among the green
tropical eyes of traders and contemplate
the subtle motion of civilization, come
sit with me once more.

            And I, novel
before my cupboard of ambitions, may
unravel suddenly in a moment.

Have we not learned from the same primer
to add, divine, and list our needs?

I sit at a linened table and the silver
and pause at the pink blood of beef
and the true calm of water. Traveler,
what have we sold more dear than
the distance between us?

5. She Becomes David

On a bright morning, I have awakened
to her bleached storm of possibilities.
She is a yawn of viral sleeplessness,
a gulf of summers sweating the brilliance
of commerce. She is a sun skirt
flaking our bereavements. And I,
in a begging of coffin silk, am turned
in my weeping away from the terrible
tread of escapade towards my own safety.
Only a prayerfull of intuition shouts
you are here now here now to be recorded.

6. Seated King

I turn the key and he awaits me there
in calm translucence waiting. He

was my sleep and fear, and now we share
the curl and doubled death of me.

He is the pampered hour that fathers cold
and warms himself glass looking at time,

the magic friend who beckons us and old
unburdenings come reveling reveling him.

TO MY CATHOLIC DAUGHTER
(on our visit to a Franciscan Monastery)

Dear child of mixed intentions,
the flowers gently cloistered at the wall
repose their still solace on the shade,
and Saint Francis bends his silent grace
above our quiet Sunday pilgrimmage.

You hesitate beneath the arc of faith,
then turn your youth into the apse
to enter the intoned mass of grief,
beyond my love and intercession:
alone among the stations of the cross.

I am divided by the image of love,
yet I have no sorrow turned to stone,
only the sin of growth and decay
turning truth to infidelities:
processional without repentance.

I stand within the cathedral of patience
and look up from these inscriptions
to meet your eyes and innocence.
The sun heals the breach between,
and you return your hand to mine.

A WREATH OF WORDS
(for Michael Joel: 1900-1955)

That room had turned sudden and strange, too still
where he died, his stilled body rolled out,
and the walls remaining high and hard
with those quick memories there. That room
straining for freedom, enclosed emptiness,
an unused form finding space too large
for practical things: a glass waiting
near its bent straw, the lamp burning
in isolation, and sheets crumbled in a quiet
corner. All those serviceable needs
for which life was made seem afraid of death.

Yet death is there, or was, because
it would not stay, having taken from its bed
the claim. And what remained was absence
of being, an early sense of past tenses.
Unsight has no use for mirrors, nor stillness
for light. Then make it dark. Give darkness
a resting place where silence may sit
unbelieving, where the night enters not,
where the night never leaves. Blackness
has its forms. Like strands over timelessness,
the forms twist inward, like wet hair
streaked over the face of silence.

Timelessness: a state beyond dimension,
like a shadow of flowers cast upon a wall
without body or hue: that almost tangible
neverthereness. Of no time now, neither
of beginning nor end. There in a suspension
of what is known, we make ourselves ready
for whispering. Our voices find slow
companions for grief. Words have their stations,

standing with us in loneliness, they come
bravely to centers of stone-marked fields
and free us into a briefly carved epitaph.
Elegies have their forms: the invocation,
the quivering threnody, the willful song
rising from emptiness to throbbing display.
Formal grief. Milton must have understood
its pastoral mending, the militant unbending
of silence. Grieving has its traditional
turns, the curve round the brink
of the void, ending in a sobbing away.
The forms bring us so quickly to the grave
that these words, still unblossomed, lie
more like a wreath of what is left unsaid,
dear Michael, so unspeakably dead.

41

I am learning to sit two
and three hours at
the water's edge.
It will be a useful
occupation.
I recall the running up
and down along
my crises. Now
I am learning to
watch water bugs and
sunlight.

COMING DOWN

1. Two weeks ago, I noted
   a pain in my groin.
   It has become mine.
        This is nothing for
   crossing continents or car pools,
   but here am I, slightly constipated,
   green with medical fears.
        Those of you in solar
   centuries to come may ask what was
   foolishness like. Here it is it is,
   a man approaching forty finds himself
        as unbelievable as the water
   that passes his eye on a picnic,
   and how the pain has made me
   larger than all the art
        of our time.

2. The other day coming up
   the midnight stairs lonely
   and lately middle aged, I
        stood at the railing wondering
   who wants this moment when
   moonlight and windows combine
   to make me singularly alert
        to my mortality. Tomorrow
   I must not forget
        the hero at breakfast.

3. On memories turning
   where I seem to reside
   among walled souvenirs,
        I think, stopping to tie
   the links between me and me,
   what right do architects have
   to plan a community, leaving out

contingencies for my mother's
accent running down the rain
after me with an extra sweater,
and the sonofabitch who chased
    us away from his troubled
world.

4. Lined up once according to size and
   the sight of Mrs. Ornstein, we followed
   each head up Seventh Street to the park
       where the man with his midwest
   tolerant smile pointed to the travelling
   farm. Here he said is the cow
   which gives milk to the city.
       The cow was large and brown
   and had very big teats.

5. The white glaze of pottery on
   my morning table is whimsical
   with the soft steam rising
       from its warm dynamic womb.
   It has a place in my eye framed
   against rosewood and green walls
   and the living reach of silver
       spoon, fork, knife, sight.
   Here I am in regular motion
   among these patterns, giving them
   time to be, but I must also be
       emphatic and arise from
   this chair leaving silence.

6. There was a hobbling man who
   still limps inside me,
   grotesque again and again
       with a carbuncle on his
   chin chin like Popeye.
   He loved Carl Hubbell

because he pitched a kingdom
       where anyone could hop
to first base.

7. Driving past the graves is asking
   whose names whose disappearances,
   and I say Michael's there
          for me as acceptable as
   buildings. Every name goes. I
   never knew my grands, but kings
   go back go back. Well
          what about it? Two
   centuries will probably review
   the row houses but whose names
   established this electric economy.
          In the grief of my
   tel-o-file, Bill Osterbeck seemed
   as alive as though I'd call
   him again as soon as
          I cross his name from
   my customer's list.

8. Screen wide in that dark well
   I made a home which still
   remains twenty five cents
          and two blocks away from
   me, and once a man with a
   striped tie stepped on stage
   and called my number out
          and gave me a red
   wagon for appearing.

9. Early love in my affection found
   me looking over her bare shoulder
   through a gauze curtain. He
          came to the window, say-
   ing he was my brother and I

was his brother. I followed him
to the garbage can in the yard
     where he searched its
galvanized depth, scattering
litter and making a private
pile of lurid magazines. I
     said, come in and meet my
wife. He said,
     after I have looked here.

10. The man in the chicken store
     prayed with my father, and for
     this I should have feared him as
          I was afraid of mystery,
     but he had blood on his apron
     and laughed with his clients,
     so I learned to talk with him.
          He saved the Sunday comics
     for me, knowing that reading
          develops a boy's mind.

11. I will populate this village. Here
     is a boy whose thick cheeks tell
     he cannot remember his name, and
          his mother makes him sit on
     the sidewalk looking at his
     hands. There is a woman coming
     out of a hallway with one leg
          thinner than a dance, and
     there at the entrance to the bank
     is the man without legs riding
     a low wooden cart on wheels. He
          is not too proud to beg
     saying, I am a cripple.

12. Time and darkness along a white
     line with coffee breaks and hot

dogs to interrupt the ride
        and change the conversation.
I am home in darkness turning
off two wide searching eyes,
and I am opening this door
        to climb the stairs to
find my bed. And I shall lie
down from my travels to sleep
when I shall sleep. It is a
        distance, more than my
time from the city
        and I am tired.

WHEN SILENCE DIVESTS ME

When silence divests me of ornament,
let me stand outside with the mourners
in the great terror of knowledge.

Let me remain like a white family
of ducks that glide on innocence
with all their energy submerged.

And where I have fallen like a tree,
may I lie in the soft decay
while I blend early into stone.

Or sometimes like a cut carrot
to be useful in some gifted way
beyond desire. Let me be

the unobserved leaf in the vast
unburden of love, more like clouds
than those which farmers see.

ON A WOUNDED MOCK ORANGE BUSH

Tucked like some obvious flags over our domains,
my mock oranges aptly decorate these shy dimensions
and subvert the landscape of my conscience.
These bushes, swaying sentinels against a common love
of a neighbor's land, swish their obsequious plots
about the boundaries of our shallow democracies
and crowd like a parade my careful freedoms.

The boy who hurdles my barberry hedge and thrusts
his innocence at private wills reduces usurpations
by one torn twig. I am framed at the window,
portrait of proprietary justice imposed on sierras
of childhood. And I remain the casualty of his retreat,
spending this victory like the sober commander
who adorns his authority with bitter silence.

Each generation learns its separateness,
subtly adopting those tortuous civil armors
which make us ponderous in springtime,
and like an accomplished general, relaxes
within the patterned movements of decades.
And liveliness survives outside our thoughts
in perennial rejeuvenation.

WOOD AND STONE

1.   Sound and Seeing

Spoken red, silent scarlet, old black,
not friends but faces,
the rage of literacy,
now's intimate
brush.
Let's go down
and enter
here.

Here at the knife edge of sound,
the pairs and thrills
and the tin thin
voice
accompanying hands
in the cradle of
ears.
Come.

Tall pillars under history
and cross rest of worship.
Three.
Three.
Nearer to vision
the turn
into
Come.

Believing that
the wind marries
that mountains
breathe
or
at least
having believed.

Now now now
concrete
and wood.
Two lighted tips
abbreviate their traffic
and mark time.
It is difficult
now.

Wood
Paper
Stone
Steel

The noon meal is simple,
yet hurried.
It is to learn
the hush
of elevators rising
in the slick sun
and to beckon airplanes
into conversations.
So I am
here.

2.   One Day

In the soft wet gutter
of me is morning.
A crow breaks my sightlessness.
A horn drives me to the urinal.
The house walks.

The garden dreams of old trees
yearning in silence,
blinking in layers.
I wear shorts, socks, shoes,
a shirt, a suit, a sign.

I and I in a
morning room.

Two boys seeking today
with bookbags and
hard-to-tie shoelaces.
One wife turning on
her rhythm.
I'll listen. I
listen.

The room is a cube
almost
in wood, and closets
hold our story. I
have the things I have. And
love is a motion
among walls.

I am a daylight button and
talking eye.
Take this down:
it is a January response
on an island breathing into
masks and coughing
at the seas.
Repeat after me:
remove your shoes and
count your fingers
and prayers. It is
a custom, a
kindness.

In the afternoon, a meeting is
inference. Who is my
friend? A friend.
And in the returning hello,

she is mine when I
sigh into a chair to
listen to the recorded
West.

I remember the taste of
fresh milk and
the bread of home.
But I am
here where my voice
is long and framed
in wood, natural
wood.

3.   Points of Interest

Jeweled foreheads in
moonlight after
the buses and words after
the shoes and gasoline. I
suppose the night is
genuine, and the light
falls on half closed
stone eyes.

And occasionally the little porcelain
on my shelf glistens
broadly on my thoughts.
I have seen their
mountain. She is
always symmetrical
in this orient of
asymmetry.

She is whiteness
in a sea of shuffling ambition,

rising out of vegetable
decay. I think each
shop owner sells
me a mountain view.
A flight.

It is there with lanterns.
Metropolitan grief,
a trolley of learning
through evenings. Two
and three, they
walk out of darkness
into the window of my
sight.

And still the shadows
in the orient's
invention. Here is
the sandman's native
place. It is a tour
out of children's
minds into carved
stone.

I had better not
loiter here for
it is considered
sacred, off the limits
of camera love. There are
thousands of stone hearts
beyond the line of
sight.

4.   The Nature of the Enemy

The smile is a vertical fence
of white, and white is
humility in vertical grains.

Eyes bend to the knees
wanting to see.

Inside inside the quiet
flower breathes and is
honored for the curve
it makes in long white
rooms, red against
natural wood.

Behind the sliding soul
the garden waters stone
and silence. Here minds
wait in adoration.

Through streets and trees
a boy on a bicycle
seeks happiness. Against
the fence the old
man eats a tangerine
and listens.

The stones are placed
where they belong.

Trees are in place.

5.   Seasonal

Winter has seemed cold
beyond memory's boding,
but flowers in spring. . . .

SOUTHERN CROSS

1. Here below where
honeysuckle covers the Jesus Saves,
a kind of speed and memory
entwined about culture,
the wizened sit upon their anecdotes
making up time.
Their eyes sunk in backed-up sorrow
wish for change without motion,
all that caution of history
crippled into a posture
of looking at dry ground
and listening to screen doors.
Here where a tangle of stores
is crucified by highways,
the young ones hold gnarled branches
reading signs and counting cars.
The multitude is here divided
into a waiting.

2. Urbanity is wilderness
which screeches for organization
and relegates the mind to shelves
of prepared indifference.
He emigrated, awakened to childhood,
to bury boredom in the continuous
detail of earth, growing multivarient
about his peaceable whimsy,
the valley nourishing desire
and seasonal endlessness.
Here between mountains in the thicket
of double negatives, he adopted
the coverall camouflage of shuffling
lithe-edged hill people to sit
with pipe and gunsight upon
the simple movements in trees.

He came upon the prayer of bullfrogs
and was saved.

3.   My rearview mirror
sees ribbons on blacktop and time,
a getting behind to distances of mind.
Here at the intersection
which is my brother's crime,
I seek the salvation of waters
and pray green weeds and woods
will restore. The silence of trees
has its station. I cut a paved swathe
through this sullen and shaken place.
The map will dedicate the backcountry
where a friend betrayed me
in this direction.

PAT

It is the isle
all green with red
necked cops
        and little men
with caps exchanging
epigrams
        in pubs
and sweet singers in
the windy tower
        and fathers with
flowing cassocks round
street corners.
        To be a tyke
or is it tike growing
up in the
elaboration
        of that meta
conceit
is it.

THE LIMITS OF INVOLVEMENT

Chairs, trees, winds, returning suns,
gentle and turbulent rains, all
practice their natural professions,
those interactions and continuings
that make my seeing transient.
I come down a quiet suburban street,
bus made and office revised and
regularly grotesque with a briefcase
full of events. I have learned
to place myself in communal traffic,
but now the steps against silence
and the moon over these houses
piquaresquely placed in urban time.

The adventure continues unto generations
of stars wound in galactic cause
and effect. Here before an intrigue
of leaves, there seems a gathering
of unlimited hordes hoarse beyond
sophistication, forceful beyond order
as life would make it, a wisdom made
of physical destiny. And these steps
promoting me into tomorrow seem
directed, not so much by a sense
of belonging, but by ever present
notions of disappearing into the night
and the memory of trees and chairs.

BENDING TREE

A tree bends my lot.
She is willed seeking the sun
bending me to her.

See her turn my view.
I cannot lace the landscape
with my morning's ease.

She has bent away.
And her turning is desire
bowing in sunlight.

Her turning is love.
In autumn shall I stake her
to the coming spring?

THE ISLAND

Somewhere
in that stopped ear,
the swim of darkness
around me,

I hear
the white bed
treading
my black house,

and alone
in the grain of
my conscience
is

childhood.

THE TOAD

That dusty grin returned, a sight
between memories of childhood
and the knowledge of dying,
breaks into my thought. Here I
am, rusted in the awakening day,
contracted in carbuncles and aches,
and grieving that time of laughter
when the whole soul of history
chronicled events that led to me,
now seated before a tactless mirror.
That ambitious wish of smoothness
hides in darkness while light lifts
its sight about my folded flesh.
It coughs and rasps in a wheezing
peregrination. Philosophy was
made to take the view of mirrors
where skin and meat are unsalted.
It is a sticky notion. I think
I'll dive below the surface.